Copyright @2024 by copywrite by Dad Is
Publisher: 3dots Publishing

www.dadisworld.com

Creative & Illustrations: Yael Eshet
Thoughts & Comments: Rachel Stein
Graphic Execution: Liron Avrami

Life Lessons from Grandpa

A Keepsake Journal

A one-of-a-kind journal of life lessons and advice –

WRITTEN BY GRANDPA!

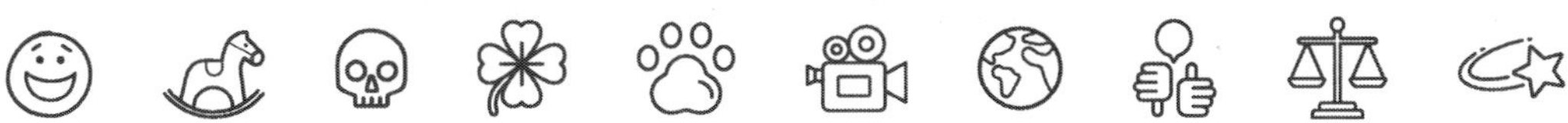

HOW TO USE THIS JOURNAL

52 significant life lessons from Grandpa to Grandchild are collected in this book.

1. *These life lessons capture the experience, knowledge, and wisdom a grandfather gathers over the years, which he wants to pass on to his family.*
2. *Covering everything from love and family to technology and happiness, this thoughtful journal addresses all the important things in life.*
3. *Each topic has plenty of space for you to create a meaningful keepsake and share everything you've learned about life with your grandchildren.*
4. *Make the life lessons uniquely yours by expressing them in your own words. Let your voice shine—be emotional, humorous, realistic—just be yourself!*

Additional pages are included to help your family get to know you, Grandpa:

1. *All About Grandpa: write down your life goals, values, achievements, and memories so your family can learn more about you!*
2. *A Grandfather's Blessings: share your heartfelt blessings with your family.*
3. *Inspire your family by creating a complete roadmap for life based on your worldview, experiences, and insights!*

 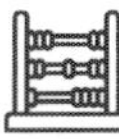       

GRANDPA'S LIFE ADVICE

CONTENTS

Grandpa's Life Advice About

WISDOM, THOUGHTS AND TIPS:

Grandpa's Life Advice About

WISDOM, THOUGHTS AND TIPS:

Grandpa's Life Advice About

WISDOM, THOUGHTS AND TIPS:

Grandpa's Life Advice About

WISDOM, THOUGHTS AND TIPS:

Grandpa's Life Advice About
CONFIDENCE

Wisdom, thoughts and tips:

Grandpa's Life Advice About

Wisdom, thoughts and tips:

Grandpa's Life Advice About

WISDOM, THOUGHTS AND TIPS:

Grandpa's Life Advice About

Wisdom, Thoughts and Tips:

Grandpa's Life Advice About DIY

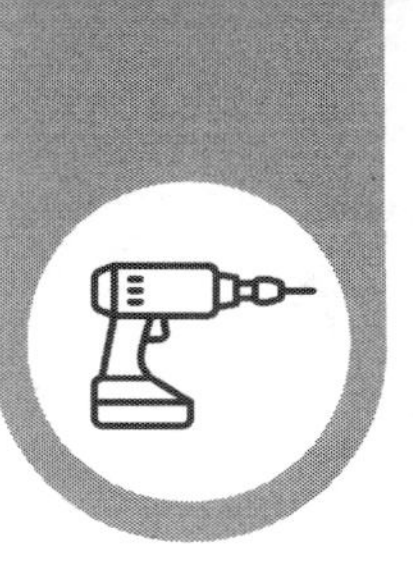

Wisdom, thoughts and tips:

Grandpa's Life Advice About

WISDOM, THOUGHTS AND TIPS:

Grandpa’s Life Advice About

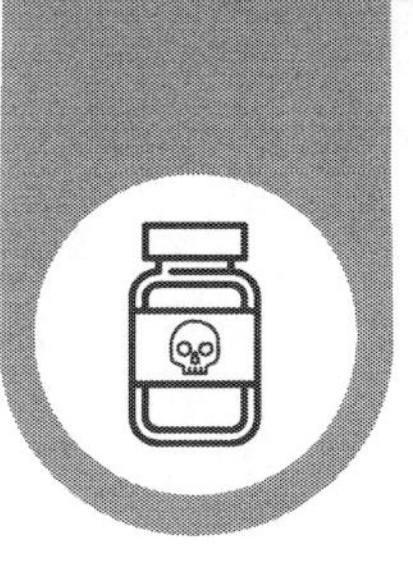

Wisdom, Thoughts and Tips:

Grandpa's Life Advice About

WISDOM, THOUGHTS AND TIPS:

Grandpa's Life Advice About

Wisdom, Thoughts and Tips:

Grandpa's Life Advice About

Wisdom, thoughts and tips:

Grandpa's Life Advice About FEAR

WISDOM, THOUGHTS AND TIPS:

Grandpa's Life Advice About

FIGHTING

Wisdom, thoughts and tips:

Grandpa's Life Advice About

FOOD

WISDOM, THOUGHTS AND TIPS:

Grandpa's Life Advice About

WISDOM, THOUGHTS AND TIPS:

Grandpa's Life Advice About

Wisdom, thoughts and tips:

Grandpa's Life Advice About
THE FUTURE

WISDOM, THOUGHTS AND TIPS:

Grandpa's Life Advice About

GOOD & BAD

Wisdom, thoughts and tips:

Grandpa's Life Advice About

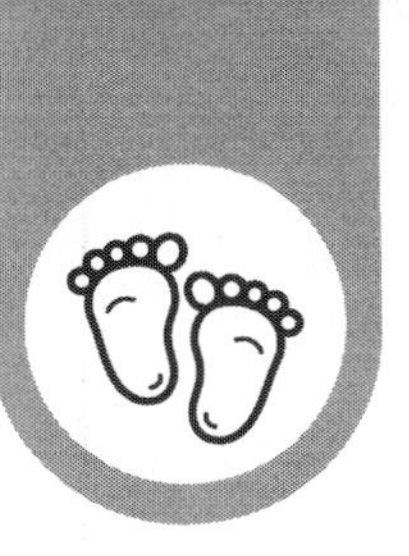

Wisdom, thoughts and tips:

Grandpa's Life Advice
About

Wisdom, Thoughts and Tips:

Grandpa's Life Advice About

WISDOM, THOUGHTS AND TIPS:

Grandpa's Life Advice About

Wisdom, thoughts and tips:

Grandpa's Life Advice About

Wisdom, thoughts and tips:

Grandpa's Life Advice About

WISDOM, THOUGHTS AND TIPS:

Grandpa's Life Advice About

Wisdom, thoughts and tips:

Grandpa's Life Advice About

WISDOM, THOUGHTS AND TIPS:

Grandpa's Life Advice About LUCK

Wisdom, thoughts and tips:

Grandpa's Life Advice About
MEMORIES

Wisdom, thoughts and tips:

Grandpa's Life Advice About

MONEY

WISDOM, THOUGHTS AND TIPS:

Grandpa's Life Advice About
MOTIVATION

Wisdom, Thoughts and Tips:

Grandpa's Life Advice About

WISDOM, THOUGHTS AND TIPS:

Grandpa's Life Advice About

WISDOM, THOUGHTS AND TIPS:

Grandpa's Life Advice About

OUTDOORS

WISDOM, THOUGHTS AND TIPS:

Grandpa's Life Advice About

WISDOM, THOUGHTS AND TIPS:

Grandpa's Life Advice About
POPULARITY

WISDOM, THOUGHTS AND TIPS:

Grandpa's Life Advice About
PROGRESS

Wisdom, thoughts and tips:

Grandpa's Life Advice About

ROLE MODELS

WISDOM, THOUGHTS AND TIPS:

Grandpa's Life Advice About

SCHOOL

Wisdom, thoughts and tips:

Grandpa's Life Advice About

SLEEP

WISDOM, THOUGHTS AND TIPS:

Grandpa's Life Advice About

WISDOM, THOUGHTS AND TIPS:

Grandpa's Life Advice About
STRENGTH

WISDOM, THOUGHTS AND TIPS:

Grandpa's Life Advice About

WISDOM, THOUGHTS AND TIPS:

Grandpa's Life Advice About

SUPERHEROS

WISDOM, THOUGHTS AND TIPS:

Grandpa's Life Advice
About
TECHNOLOGY

Wisdom, thoughts and tips:

Grandpa's Life Advice About

WISDOM, THOUGHTS AND TIPS:

Grandpa's Life Advice About

TOYS

WISDOM, THOUGHTS AND TIPS:

Grandpa's Life Advice About

TRAVEL

WISDOM, THOUGHTS AND TIPS:

Grandpa's Life Advice About

WISDOM, THOUGHTS AND TIPS:

Grandpa's Life Advice About

OUR WORLD

WISDOM, THOUGHTS AND TIPS:

ALL ABOUT GRANDPA

CONTENTS

My Biggest Achievements

The moments and accomplishments I'm most proud of and what they mean to me

My Life Goals

The dreams and aspirations I've set for myself, and the journey I'm on to achieve them

What I've Learned as a Grandfather

Reflections on the joys and challenges of being a grandparent and how it has changed me

My Best Childhood Memories

A few of my most memorable experiences and memories as a kid

....

....

....

....

....

....

....

....

....

....

....

....

....

My values

The core beliefs and principles that guide my decisions and shape who I am

....

....

....

....

....

....

....

....

....

....

....

....

....

My Favorite Family Traditions

Special family traditions that mean a lot to me and bring us closer together

The Things I Love Most

A collection of the people, places, and things that bring me the greatest joy

What Makes Me Proud

The things that fill me with pride,
from my achievements to the people I love

....

....

....

....

....

....

....

....

....

....

....

....

....

A Grandfather's Blessings

Take a moment to share your heartfelt blessings with your grandchildren and family. Write words of love, encouragement, and hope for their future.

Whether it's expressing your wishes for their joy and success, sharing hopes for their happiness, or reflecting on the values you hold dear, let this be a personal message they can cherish forever.

Write your blessings on the next page:

Dear family, grandchildren and loved ones,

Love, Grandpa

Visit our website

www.dadisworld.com

IF YOU WANT MORE

Scan to Visit Store

Made in the USA
Columbia, SC
20 June 2025

fde45c84-40aa-480a-8d63-1ed1bc60725fR02